S0-BQZ-276

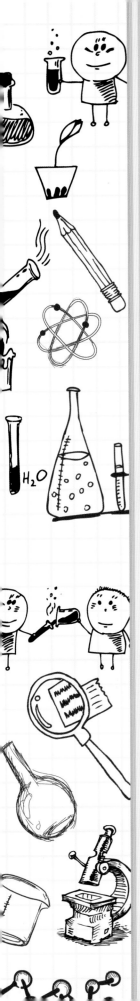

Learning Playground

Fun with Cultural Crafts and Performing Arts

WORLD BOOK

a Scott Fetzer company
Chicago

www.worldbookonline.com

World Book, Inc.
233 N. Michigan Avenue
Chicago, IL 60601
U.S.A.

For information about other World Book publications, visit our website at **http://www.worldbookonline.com** or call **1-800-WORLDBK (967-5325)**.

For information about sales to schools and libraries, call **1-800-975-3250 (United States)**; **1-800-837-5365 (Canada)**.

Library of Congress Cataloging-in-Publication Data

Fun with cultural crafts and performing arts.
  p. cm. -- (Learning playground)
  Includes index.
  Summary: "An activity-based volume that introduces cultural crafts and performing arts from around the world. Features include a glossary, an additional resource list, and an index"--Provided by publisher.
  ISBN 978-0-7166-0227-9
  1. Handicraft--Juvenile literature. 2. Ethnic art--Juvenile literature. 3. Ethnic performing arts--Juvenile literature. I. World Book, Inc.
  TT160.F87 2011
  790.1--dc22
                    2011004730

STAFF

Executive Committee
President: Donald D. Keller
Vice President and
  Editor in Chief: Paul A. Kobasa
Vice President, Marketing/
  Digital Products: Sean Klunder
Vice President, International: Richard Flower
Director, Human Resources: Bev Ecker

Editorial
Associate Manager, Supplementary
  Publications: Cassie Mayer
Editor: Shawn Brennan
Researcher: Annie Brodsky
Manager, Contracts & Compliance
  (Rights & Permissions): Loranne K. Shields
Indexer: David Pofelski

Graphics and Design
Manager: Tom Evans
Coordinator, Design Development and
  Production: Brenda B. Tropinski
Senior Designer: Isaiah Sheppard
Associate Designer: Matt Carrington
Photographs Editor: Kristine Strom

Pre-Press and Manufacturing
Director: Carma Fazio
Manufacturing Manager: Barbara Podczerwinski
Production/Technology Manager:
  Anne Fritzinger

Learning Playground
Set ISBN: 978-0-7166-0225-5

Printed in Malaysia by TWP Sdn Bhd, Johor Bahru
1st printing July 2011

Acknowledgments:
The publishers gratefully acknowledge the following sources for photography. All illustrations were prepared by WORLD BOOK unless otherwise noted.

Cover: 4CornersImages/eStock Photo; Lebrecht Music and Arts Photo Library/Alamy Images; Shutterstock

Christine Osborne Pictures/Alamy Images 37; Lebrecht Music and Arts Photo Library/Alamy Images 25; Buddy Mays, Alamy Images 24; Photo Japan/Robert Harding Picture Library/Alamy Images 16, 17; AP Photo 46; Upperhall/Robert Harding World Imagery/Getty Images 56; Farley Baricuatro 14; Dreamstime 4, 5, 6, 16, 17, 19, 36, 42, 56, 57, 58; Danita Delimont, Gallo Images/Getty Images 24; Siri Stafford, Getty Images 33; iStockphoto 7, 23, 59; Shutterstock 4, 5, 9, 11, 12, 16, 17, 32, 33, 36, 37, 42, 43, 47, 48; Design Pics/SuperStock 7; The Irish Image Collection/SuperStock 44; Audrey Tropinski 13.

Table of Contents

There is a glossary on page 62. Terms defined in the glossary are in type that **looks like this** on their first appearance on any spread (two facing pages).

What Are Crafts and Performing Arts?

Pottery is a type of decorative art or craft made of baked clay.

People around the world have long made beautiful things with their hands. To make these beautiful things, people developed special skills. A trade or art that requires special skill is called a craft. Paper folding, paper cutting, weaving, quilting, and **pottery** are all crafts. And there are many more.

Craftworkers make objects that people use in their daily life. The objects they make are useful and beautiful to look at and to touch because of the workers' skill. Each object is a work of art.

Most crafts are activities that have been done for a very long time. Some craftmaking has been handed down through generations. Some crafts developed in different parts of the world at the same time.

In many parts of the world, people hand-weave such textiles as rugs, blankets, and clothing.

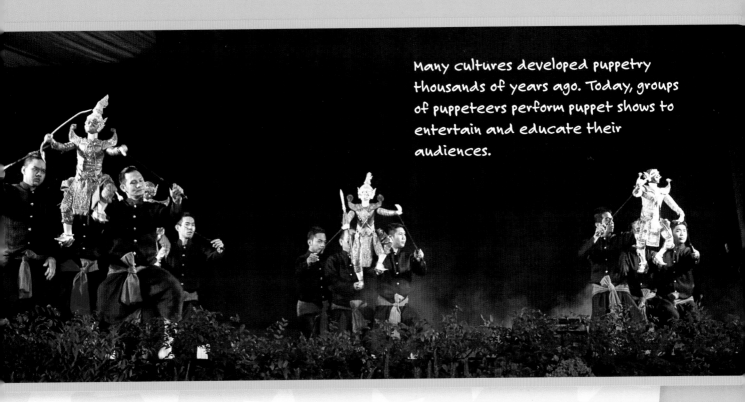

Many cultures developed puppetry thousands of years ago. Today, groups of puppeteers perform puppet shows to entertain and educate their audiences.

People around the world have special ways of expressing themselves through other types of art too, such as music, dance, and theater. These are called the performing arts. Many groups of people have had their own special types of music, dance, and theater for a very long time.

This book includes crafts and performing arts projects from around the world that you can do. But before you begin each project, be sure to read all the directions and gather all the materials you will need. Then have fun creating and performing!

Performances by the Ballet Folklórico de México display Mexican cultural traditions.

Many people enjoy sewing clothes and such household articles as bedspreads, pillows, curtains, and slipcovers.

In Stitches

There are huge machines in factories that sew most of our clothes and other items. But many people enjoy sewing by hand or with their own sewing machines. Some people like to sew special things for their homes, such as curtains or pillows. People also sew gifts for their friends or families.

The first settlers in America, called colonists, had no factories or shops, and many communities had no craftworkers either. People had to build their own houses, grow their own food, and make their own clothes. Since cloth was scarce, colonists saved old clothes even when they became ragged. They took old pieces of cloth and pieced them together to make blankets called patchwork quilts. The craft of quilt-making is still popular today.

Embroidery (ehm BROY duhr ee) is a craft that is related to sewing. It is used mainly for decoration. A person who embroiders uses a special needle and colored thread called embroidery floss to make different kinds of stitches on cloth. The stitches can form pictures or designs.

Since prehistoric times, most cultures have developed their own embroidery styles. People embroider clothing and use embroidered furnishings to decorate their homes and public buildings.

In some cultures, people use elaborate embroidery designs to decorate clothing.

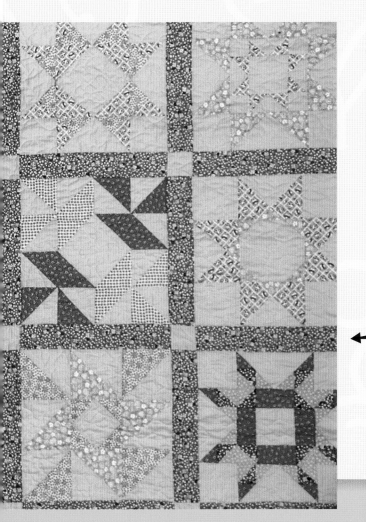

Today, quilters combine traditional patterns and techniques with a fresh approach to produce unique designs.

BASIC STITCHING

Before you **embroider**, practice basic stitching.

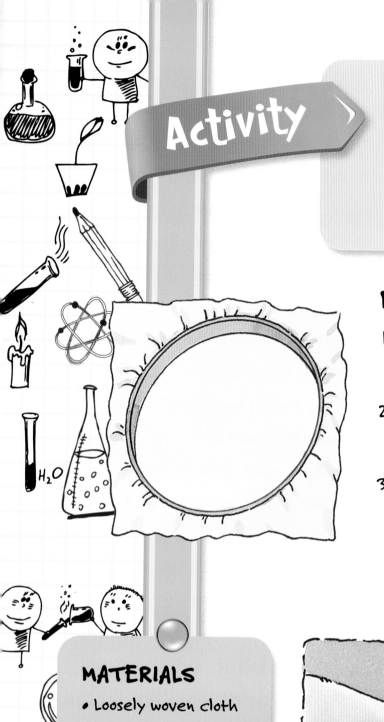

DIRECTIONS

1. Pull a piece of cloth between the two parts of the embroidery hoop.

2. Draw a simple design on the cloth with a pencil.

3. Cut a piece of floss as long as your arm from fingertips to elbow. Moisten one end and push it through the eye of the needle. Tie a knot, as shown below, in the other end of the floss.

MATERIALS

- Loosely woven cloth
- Embroidery hoop
- Pencil
- Embroidery floss (from a fabric or arts and crafts shop)
- Embroidery needle
- Scissors

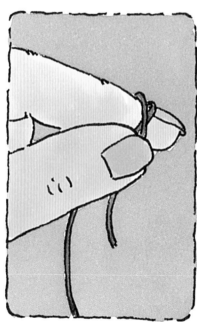
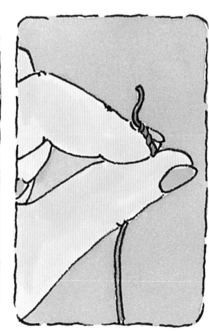

4. Push the needle up through a part of your design on the cloth. Pull the needle out on the other side until all the floss except the knot comes through. Then push the needle back down and pull the floss through. You should now have one stitch. Make a row of stitches all the same length.

5. When you are almost at the end of your floss, push the needle through to the back of the cloth. Make two small stitches, one on top of the other. Slide the needle under the stitches and pull the floss through. Cut the floss.

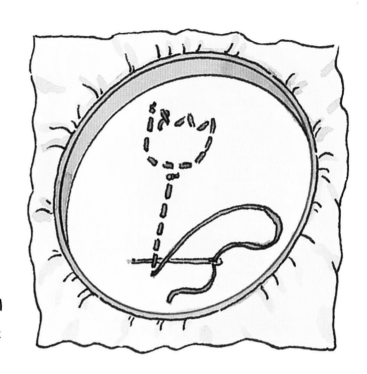

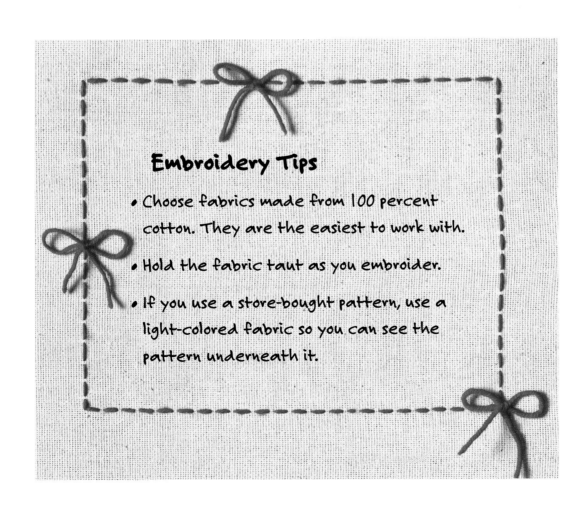

Embroidery Tips

- Choose fabrics made from 100 percent cotton. They are the easiest to work with.

- Hold the fabric taut as you embroider.

- If you use a store-bought pattern, use a light-colored fabric so you can see the pattern underneath it.

LEARN TO EMBROIDER

Why did colonial women make so many decorations with needlework? They used it to cover holes and rips in old clothing and linens while decorating the cloth at the same time. You, too, can do **embroidery** to make cloth as pretty as a picture.

MATERIALS

- Loosely woven cloth
- Embroidery hoop
- Pencil
- Embroidery floss
- Embroidery needle
- Scissors

DIRECTIONS

1. Place your cloth in an embroidery hoop.

2. On the cloth, draw a design with large and small flowers. Then embroider the design with the following stitches:

3. Use the satin stitch for filling in large petals and leaves.

4. Use the chain stitch to make stems.

Satin stitch

Chain stitch

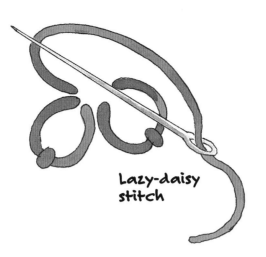

5. Use the lazy-daisy stitch to outline tiny petals and leaves.

Lazy-daisy stitch

6. Knotted stitches, like the ones in the center of this flower (right), are easy to make. Wrap the floss around the point of the needle three times. Push the needle with the loops back in next to the hole where you pulled out the needle.

Traditional Slovakian costumes have intricate embroidery designs.

USE BATIK TO MAKE A PICTURE

People around the world have been dyeing cloth for thousands of years. In many places, special ways of dyeing have developed. For example, in Indonesia people use a method called **batik** (BUH teek).

Batik is a method of applying colored designs to fabric. A design is made on the fabric, and those sections that are not to be dyed are covered with wax or other substance that will not absorb the dye. When the wax has hardened, the fabric can be dipped into a dye, or the dye can be applied with a paint brush. The covered parts resist the dye. After the cloth is dry, the wax can be removed by boiling the cloth.

Using a white crayon and watercolor paints, you can create your own batik on paper.

Melted wax is applied to cloth with a paint brush.

Dyes are applied to the fabric with a paint brush after the wax has hardened. ➡

DIRECTIONS

1. Put on the apron, smock, or T-shirt to protect your clothes. Cover your workspace with newspaper.

2. Using the white crayon, draw a picture on the paper. Wherever you draw with the crayon, the paint will not absorb into the paper.

3. When you have finished putting in the linework of your picture, you can begin to add the paint. As you brush the paint over the crayon, notice how it resists the color.

   If you have trouble seeing the white crayon on the white paper, you can lightly sketch your design with a pencil first.

MATERIALS

- Apron, smock, or old T-shirt
- Newspaper
- Watercolor paper or a similar heavy paper
- White crayon
- Watercolor paints
- Paint brush
- Small container for water

Allow your picture to dry thoroughly before you display it!

Activity

WEAVE A PAPER MAT

The Samals are a group of people in the Philippines who weave beautiful mats. They use the leaves of the pandanus (pan DAY nuhs) plant, which grows in the region. You can weave a mat from materials around you, too. Try this activity to make a mat out of magazine pages.

Samal mats often feature brilliant colors.

DIRECTIONS

1. Have an adult remove staples from eight bound, two-page magazine spreads.

2. Fold one spread lengthwise. Open it and cut it along the fold. Repeat this with the other sheets to make 16 pieces.

3. Fold one piece in half lengthwise. Fold it in half lengthwise again. Press the paper firmly into a long flat strip. Fold and press the other pieces the same way.

MATERIALS

- 8 colorful two-page spreads pulled from large magazines of the same size
- Staple remover
- Scissors
- Clear tape

4. Place 8 strips side by side. These up-and-down strips are called the warp. Tape the ends of the strips together on one side and then tape them to your work table.

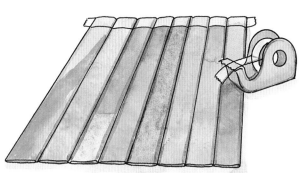

5. Weave the remaining strips over and under the taped ones. The strips that go across are called the weft. The first, third, fifth, and seventh strips should go over and then under. The second, fourth, sixth, and eighth strips should go under and then over.

6. Slide the strips as closely together as possible.

7. Finish your mat by taping the strips together on all four edges of your mat. Start with the side opposite the one that's taped to your work surface. Trim the edges so the sides are even, or keep the edges fringed.

Use your artwork as a place mat at your next meal. Or display it where everyone can enjoy it!

Praying
mantis

OriGaMi

Crane

Have you ever made a paper airplane? If you have, you have enjoyed the craft called **origami** (AWR uh GAH mee).

Originally, the Japanese invented about 100 origami figures. Most are natural forms, such as birds, frogs, and fish. One form of origami, with shapes all its own, is called noshi (NOH shee). These are pleated paper decorations that Japanese people attach to gifts.

The Japanese like to use squares of paper for origami. The squares range from 6 to 10 inches (15 to 25 centimeters) in size. They also use a special paper called washi (WAH shee).

Owl

To make washi, bark is washed and mixed with a gluelike substance. Then a special screen is dipped into the pulp.

Fish

Papermaking families in Japan still make washi by hand. To make washi, they first mix a gluelike liquid with bark, cotton, linen, or tree fibers and stir the mixture into a mush called pulp.

Next they dip a special screen into the pulp and drain out most of the moisture. Then they place the wet sheets on a flat surface to dry. The Japanese use the washi to make umbrellas, kites, and origami.

Girl

Flowers

Frog

Wet washi sheets are dried on a flat surface.

MAKE ORIGAMI PAPER DOLLS

Origami is enjoyed all around the world today. People in many countries have added new designs to the ones first created in Japan. Here are instructions for how to make paper dolls. Use them as puppets or as decorations for packages, or write names on them and use them as place cards for family meals.

DIRECTIONS

1. Fold a square of paper in half from corner to corner to make a crease that marks the center of the paper. Unfold the square.

2. Fold the sides to the center.

3. Fold the bottom up. Now you have a triangle of paper.

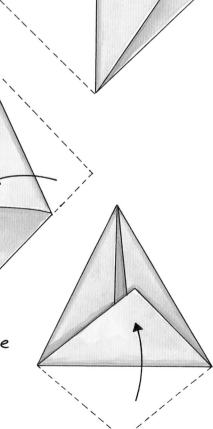

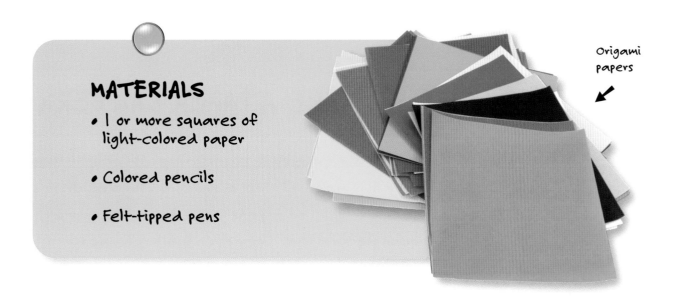

MATERIALS

- 1 or more squares of light-colored paper

- Colored pencils

- Felt-tipped pens

Origami papers

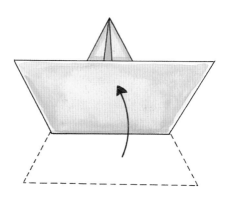

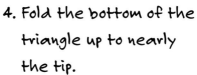

4. Fold the bottom of the triangle up to nearly the tip.

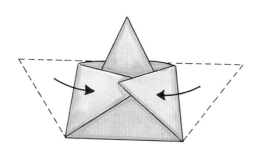

5. Turn the paper over and fold the doll arms in toward the center.

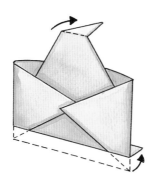

6. Fold the tip back. Then fold the base back to make the doll stand upright.

7. Draw a face on the doll and some designs on the body.

MAKE A PAPER LANTERN

A lantern is a case that covers a candle or light bulb. Usually it is made of glass or paper through which the light can shine. The Japanese use paper lanterns as colorful decorations. They even have a name for making lanterns—kerigami (kehr uh GAH mee), the Japanese word for cutting paper. To make your own kerigami lanterns, follow these steps.

MATERIALS

- Sheets of heavy paper in different colors
- Pencil
- Ruler
- Scissors
- Clear tape
- Tissue paper, the same size as the heavy paper
- Hole punch
- Thin string or thread

DIRECTIONS

1. To make the center tube, cut a couple of inches off the long side of a sheet of heavy paper. Overlap the edges of the paper and tape them together.

2. Fold another sheet of the heavy paper in half lengthwise. Using the ruler, draw a line the length of the paper about an inch (2 centimeters) from the edges away from the fold.

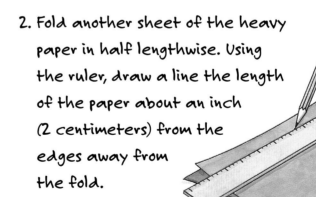

3. Cut slits about 0.5 inches (1.25 centimeters) apart up to this line. Unfold the slotted paper.

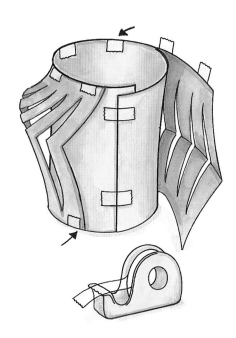

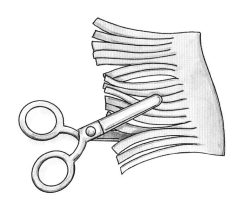

4. Tape the top and bottom edges of the slotted paper to the tube so that the slotted paper bows out at the fold.

5. Fold a sheet of tissue paper with the short sides together. Cut the bottom edge with the fold to the left to make a fringe. Open the paper and tape it to the inside of the lantern.

6. Punch two holes at the top of the lantern, across from each other. Fasten a line of string across a porch or other outdoor area. Run a shorter string through the holes of the lantern and tie a knot to fasten around the longer line of string. Make more lanterns if you wish, and fasten these to the line. Watch the fringe wave in the breeze.

PAPER CUTTING

Cutting paper to make beautiful designs is a craft in many parts of the world. A kind of paper cutting called papel picado (puh PEHL pih KAH doh) is a popular craft in the Mexican state of Puebla. The markets there offer hundreds of scary and funny characters cut into paper banners. Mexicans hang papel picado banners on string to decorate their homes and shops. You, too, can cut paper and make a colorful decoration. Just follow these steps.

MATERIALS

- Light-colored pencil or crayon
- Sheet of heavy black paper
- Scissors
- Tissue paper in different colors
- Glue or tape
- String
- Hole punch

DIRECTIONS

1. Draw a large fish or some other animal on the sheet of black paper.

2. Draw shapes on your animal. You need to make the shapes big enough to cut easily.

3. Cut out the animal and the inside shapes. To do this, you may fold the paper a little and make a small slit in the fold. Poke the blade of your scissors through the slit. Hold the scissors in one place and move the paper as you cut.

Papel picado is used as a decoration for celebrations in many Central and South American countries.

4. Cover the cutouts with different-colored tissue paper. Glue or tape the tissue in place.

5. Punch a hole in the top of your decoration and loop a string through the hole.

If you hang your paper cutout in front of a window, the light will shine through and brighten the room.

Many Native Americans today continue the tradition of pottery-making.

Native American Pottery

Native Americans created many different kinds of beautiful **pottery.** They made most of their pottery by rolling pieces of clay into slender strips, then laying them on top of one another in a spiraling, ropelike coil. The artist sometimes kept the coils on the pottery as decoration but often scraped the surface smooth.

The Inca often painted their pottery with geometric patterns, as seen on this bottle.

The Inca of South America made some of the finest pottery in the New World. (North, Central, and South America are sometimes called the New World). The Aztec of Mexico and the Maya of Central America and southern Mexico painted some of their pottery with scenes of religious ceremonies. In North America, the early Indians in what is now the southwestern United States made fine bowls and jars. Many of these were in the shape of animals.

Some Native Americans still make beautiful pottery today. The Hopi of northern Arizona are excellent potters.

Zuni bowl

Prehistoric Pueblo lamp

Hopi bowl

Prehistoric water jar

MAKE PLAY CLAY

To make your own claylike dough, follow this recipe.

DIRECTIONS

1. Put on the apron, smock, or T-shirt to protect your clothes. Cover your workspace with newspaper.

2. Mix the flour, salt, water, oil, and cream of tartar in the saucepan.

3. Ask an adult to cook the mixture over low heat until thick. Then add food coloring until the dough is the color you want.

4. Let the dough cool. Then place it on the pastry board. Work the dough back and forth with your knuckles and palms.

5. Store the dough in a closed plastic bag at room temperature.

When you are ready to sculpt, your "clay" will be ready, too!

MATERIALS

- Apron, smock, or old T-shirt
- Newspaper
- Saucepan
- 1 cup flour
- 1/2 cup salt
- 1 cup water
- 1 tablespoon oil
- 1 teaspoon cream of tartar
- Food coloring
- Spoon
- Pastry board
- Plastic bag that seals closed

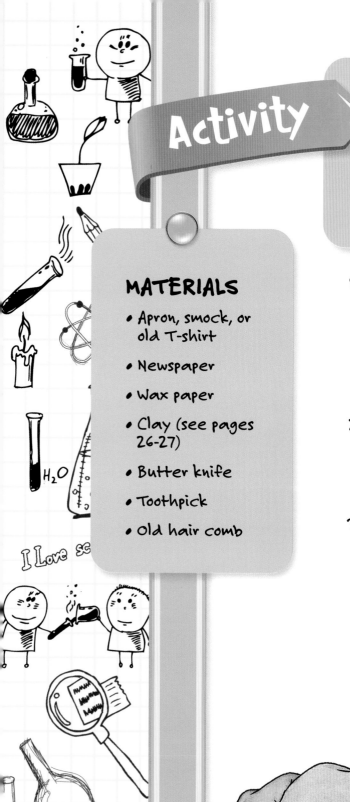

PLAY WITH CLAY

Playing with clay is fun! Experiment with it. Try these exercises to prepare for making a coil bowl.

MATERIALS

- Apron, smock, or old T-shirt
- Newspaper
- Wax paper
- Clay (see pages 26-27)
- Butter knife
- Toothpick
- Old hair comb

DIRECTIONS

1. Put on the apron, smock, or T-shirt to protect your clothes. Cover your workspace with newspaper.

2. Work with your clay on wax paper. This way you can easily move your finished model somewhere to dry.

3. To cut off workable sections of the clay, use a butter knife. Shape the clay into a round ball. Pass the ball between your hands. Use your palms to press against the clay and push out any air bubbles inside the clay. If the clay is drying too fast, you can add a little bit of water to your hands to help shape the clay.

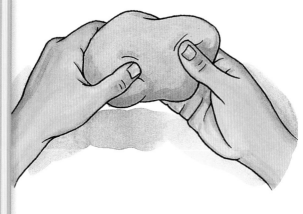
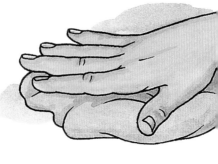

4. To make a coil, cut off a section of the clay and roll it between the palms of your hands. Roll the coil with both hands from the center to the ends until it is the thickness and length you want. (Be sure to press evenly throughout the coil. Pressing too hard can cause the coil to get too thin.) Repeat until you have several coils to practice with.

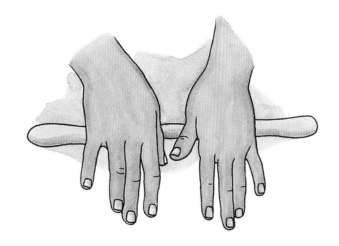

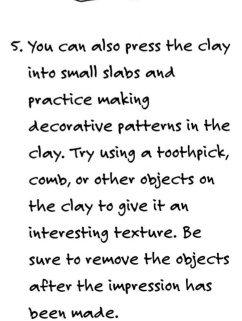

5. You can also press the clay into small slabs and practice making decorative patterns in the clay. Try using a toothpick, comb, or other objects on the clay to give it an interesting texture. Be sure to remove the objects after the impression has been made.

Activity ›

MAKE A CLAY POT

Now that you know how to make clay coils, try working them into a pot. You can make a clay pot the same way the Native Americans did.

MATERIALS

- Apron, smock, or old T-shirt
- Newspaper
- Baking sheet
- Clay (see pages 26-27)
- Water
- Plastic sheet
- Acrylic paints
- Paintbrush
- Craft stick

DIRECTIONS

1. Put on the apron, smock, or T-shirt to protect your clothes. Cover your workspace with newspaper. Work with your clay on wax paper. This way, you can easily move your finished model somewhere to dry.

2. Roll out a snake of clay about 1 inch (2.5 centimeters) thick.

3. Coil the clay snake into a spiral base for the clay pot. Make the base about 4 inches (10 centimeters) wide.

4. Roll out more snakes of clay. Lay a coil on the top of the base, around the edges, bringing the two ends of the snake of clay together, pinching off any extra clay.

5. Build the walls of the pot upwards by layering coils of clay, one on top of the other.

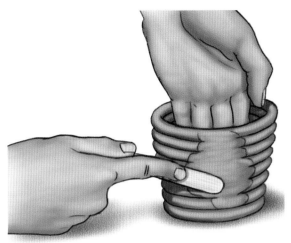

6. When the pot is the size and shape you want, smooth the outer part of the clay pot using water on the hands to rub each coil section together. This binds the clay and makes the pot strong. You can use a craft stick or your finger to help smooth the edges of the coils together. Place a hand inside the pot while pressing on the outside to prevent the walls from collapsing.

7. Leave your pot to dry over a couple of days. When your pot has dried completely, you may draw designs on it with acrylic paints.

Tips for Making Your Pot

- If your pot collapses as you build the coil walls, mash the coils into a ball, knead out the air bubbles, and begin again.

- If you are working with natural clay, score (scratch) the top of each coil with a toothpick or other sharp object. Then lightly dampen the coils with water before you attach them. This will help form a "glue" to keep the coils together.

- If you are using natural clay and you live near a **pottery** studio, you may be able to bring your pot there to be fired in a kiln. Do not paint your bowl with acrylics if you plan to fire it. Also, be sure to knead out any air bubbles from the clay before you make your coils. Otherwise, your pot may explode in the kiln!

During Chinese New Year, Chinese communities around the world perform dances featuring colorful dragon and lion costumes.

Celebrating with Crafts

Many countries have their own ways of celebrating special events or religious holidays. Some people celebrate happy events by decorating their homes and streets, wearing special clothes, and exchanging gifts. Many of these celebrations include special meals, dancing, and parades.

A **piñata** (pee NYAH tah) is used in many celebrations in Mexico. A piñata is a brightly decorated paper or clay figure containing candy, fruit, or small toys. The piñata may be shaped like an animal, an elf, a star, or some other object. Many people play a game with piñatas at children's birthday parties and other celebrations. In Mexico, children play with a piñata each night on the nine evenings before Christmas.

A piñata is hung above the children's heads. The children then take turns trying to hit the piñata with a stick while their eyes are covered with a blindfold. When someone breaks the piñata, the things inside it fall out. The children then scramble to collect as many things as they can hold.

Piñatas are popular features at birthday parties and other celebrations in many parts of the world.

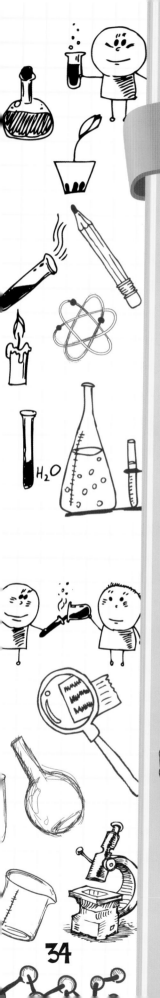

Activity > MAKE AN OWL PIÑATA

Many artists use **papier-mâché** (PAY puhr muh SHAY) to make sculptures. Papier-mâché can be made with newspaper mixed with paste. Papier-mâché is easy to press into shape when it is wet, and it becomes very hard when it dries. Find out for yourself how to work with papier-mâché. Try making an owl **piñata.**

DIRECTIONS

1. Put on the apron, smock, or T-shirt to protect your clothes. Cover your workspace with newspaper.

2. Mix two parts glue with one part warm water in a bowl. Stir well.

3. Blow up the balloon, knot it, and rub it with the oil.

4. Tear the newspaper into strips about one inch (about 2.5 centimeters) wide. Dip the strips into the glue mixture. Cover the balloon, except for the knot, with a layer of strips going in one direction. Then cover the first layer with a second layer going in another direction. Apply three or four layers of this papier-mâché.

5. Let the balloon dry for 24 hours.

6. Burst the balloon at the knot and pull it free. Ask an adult to use the nail and hammer to make two small holes about one inch (about 2.5 centimeters) apart at the top of the piñata. Run a long piece of string through the holes and tie its ends.

7. Fill the hollow papier-mâché with candy and tiny toys. Close the hole where the knot was with masking tape.

8. To make feathers, cut a fringe on one side of the streamers. Put glue on the unfringed side of the streamers and wind them around the owl. Draw eyes and a beak on construction paper. Cut them out and glue them to the owl.

MATERIALS

- Apron, smock, or old T-shirt
- Newspaper
- Sponge
- White glue
- Warm water
- Bowl
- Large balloon
- Cooking oil
- Wrapped candy and tiny toys
- Masking tape
- Scissors
- Orange and brown paper streamers
- Construction paper
- Nail and hammer
- String

Symphony orchestras play all types of music, but most specialize in classical works.

Music Around the World

Good times everywhere are even better with music. But the sound of music can be different from place to place. Why? Because orchestras (AWR kuh struhz) and bands in different parts of the world play different kinds of instruments.

For example, in North America and western Europe, many people like big bands with **brass** instruments.

New Orleans is often considered the birthplace of jazz. Today, New Orleans jazz musicians frequently perform in public spaces around the city.

Gamelan is a traditional Indonesian orchestra mainly made up of **percussion** instruments.

In Mexico, people of all ages enjoy mariachi (MAHR ee AHCH ee) bands with acoustic guitars and accordions (uh KAWR dee uhnz)—keyboard instruments that you squeeze to make sounds. Farther south in Ecuador, the Native American musicians of the Andes Mountains play panpipes and marimbas (muh RIHM buhz).

In China, musical groups play bells, drums, gongs, flutes, and stringed instruments called the quin (chihn) and the pipa (PEE pah). In Japan, special musical groups called gagaku (gah GAH koo) also play bells, drums, gongs, flutes, and their own kinds of ancient stringed instruments. In Indonesia, the popular gamelan (GUHM uh lahn) orchestra includes many instruments that are played by striking them.

The first electric guitars were developed in the 1930's. Today, most rock groups are based around the electric guitar.

Also, many young people around the world listen to rock groups with electric guitars and synthesizers (SIHN thuh SY zuhrz).

MAKE MUSICAL INSTRUMENTS

Follow these instructions to make musical instruments of your own!

MATERIALS

- Sturdy box
- Wrapping paper
- Tape
- Large and small rubber bands

RUBBER-BAND STRUMMER

Historians believe that the guitar originated in Africa. Today, this popular stringed instrument is played all over the world. Follow these instructions to make your own simple guitar.

DIRECTIONS

1. To decorate the box, cover it inside and out with wrapping paper.

2. Wrap 3-4 rubber bands around the box. You can change the sound by altering rubber bands. The smaller and tighter the rubber band, the higher the sound it makes.

3. When you find notes that sound good together, try strumming a melody.

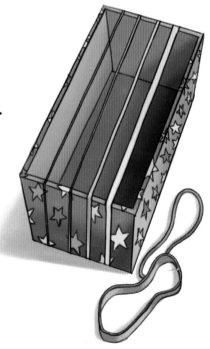

COFFEE-CAN BONGOS

Bongos are similar to the tabla (TAH blah), an instrument played in India. The tabla sometimes includes two drums, one played with the right hand and the other with the left hand. What other kinds of drums do you know?

MATERIALS

- 2 empty coffee cans—
  1 large, 1 small, with lids
- Wrapping paper
- Duck tape or packing tape
- Construction paper
- Glue

DIRECTIONS

1. Wrap the cans with wrapping paper to decorate them.

2. Snap the lids onto the cans. Then turn the cans upside down on a table.

3. Have a friend hold the cans while you tape them together. Wind two or three layers of tape around the cans. Then turn the cans right-side up. If you want to, you can decorate the tape with stars or other designs that you cut out of the construction paper.

4. To play the bongos, sit on a chair or on the floor and hold them between your knees. Tap each drum with your fingertips. The smaller drum will make a higher sound than the larger one.

MAKE MUSICAL INSTRUMENTS

MARACAS

Maracas are **percussion** instruments of Native American origin. They consist of seeds or pebbles enclosed in a dry gourd or gourd-shaped body and shaken like a rattle. Maracas are usually played in pairs. Follow these instructions to make your own maracas!

MATERIALS

- 2 small plastic bottles with caps
- Rice, macaroni, or beans
- Masking tape
- Markers

DIRECTIONS

1. Put some rice, macaroni, or beans into a plastic bottle. Screw on the cap.

2. Wrap the entire bottle with masking tape so that you cannot see what is inside of it. Be careful not to cover the cap.

3. Using the markers, draw designs on the bottle.

   Now you are ready to shake, rattle, and roll! You can change the sound by adding or subtracting rice, macaroni, or beans.

MATERIALS

- Cardboard paper-towel tube
- Wax paper
- Pencil
- Rubber band
- Scissors

CARDBOARD FLUTE

Asian Indians play an instrument called the bansuri (ban SUHR ee). The bansuri is a simple flute made from bamboo. It uses no keys and requires careful fingering on its six or seven holes. Make your own cardboard flute and enjoy!

DIRECTIONS

1. Use a pencil to poke holes along one side of a cardboard tube.

2. Cover one end of the tube with a piece of wax paper.

3. Hold the wax paper in place with a rubber band, as shown.

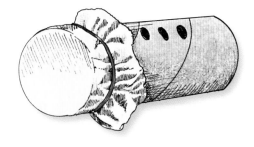

Hum into the uncovered end of the tube as you move your fingers over the holes. Toot, toot! You're playing a tune on your own flute.

Moving to the Music

Drums and bright, colorful costumes are common features of African dance.

Dance is one of the oldest forms of art. People dance to express themselves, for religious reasons, to celebrate their culture, to be with other people, for exercise, or just to have fun!

Religious dances are forms of prayer. Native Americans may dance to ask for help in hunting, farming, or war. They may imitate animals by moving like them or wearing masks. **Folk dance** celebrates a group's history and traditions. Folk dancers may wear colorful costumes. Many folk dances are easy to learn. People may join hands or move in a circle. Other folk dances are full of energy and passion and the dancers must be very athletic.

Whirling dervishes dance to the music of a reed pipe as part of their worship of the Islamic religion.

We may go to a theater to see dancers who have been specially trained to perform a kind of dance. Ballet is the oldest kind of dance performed in theaters. It began in the 1400's at the courts of princes, dukes, and other rulers in what is now Italy. For hundreds of years, ballet dancers have made beautiful movements as they leap and twirl across the stage.

Ballet is a form of theatrical dance that uses set movements and poses that display elegance and grace.

Indian folk dance features elaborate costuming and bodily decoration, such as ankle bells, shining head pieces, and beautiful robes.

LEARN AN IRISH JIG

Folk dances are performed by ordinary people. All people, from farmers to city workers, enjoy moving to the beat of their favorite music. Every country has certain dances that belong to its people.

An Irish jig is a popular European folk dance that features rapid footwork. Follow these instructions to learn the basic steps of a simple Irish jig.

Irish jigs are lively dances performed to folk music.

DIRECTIONS

1. Stand on your left leg, pointing your right foot in front of it.

2. Raise your right foot so that it is in line with your left knee.

3. Bring your right foot to your left knee. At the same time, hop on your left leg.

4. Hop again as you move your right foot behind your left leg.

5. Point your left foot in front of you and do the steps in reverse!

Tips for Doing the Jig

- Wear heeled shoes.
- Keep your hands and arms straight along your sides.
- Keep your weight on the ball of your foot.

Theater Around the World

People all around the world love going to the theater. Theater is a type of entertainment that includes plays and other stage performances. A theater is also the building in which such performances take place. Most big cities have many theater buildings. Different styles of theater exist all over the world.

Western theater is a style of storytelling that began in ancient Greece. Stories of comedy and tragedy came from the ancient Greeks. Comedies are funny. Tragedies are sad. Western theater also followed the Greek custom of dividing stories into parts called acts.

The new Globe Theatre opened in London in 1997. It is a replica of the one in which William Shakespeare began presenting his plays about 1599.

Theater from the eastern part of the world, such as from Asia, is very different and tells stories in other ways.

Theater in India goes back about 2,000 years. Stories told in Indian theaters are like long poems. And all Indian plays have happy endings.

Chinese theater is about 800 years old. China's most popular form of play today is Peking opera (OP uhr uh). Its plays are based on Chinese stories, history, and folklore. Actors may change or make up their lines as they go along.

In Peking opera, special props—the objects that the actors use onstage—are the only clues to where a play takes place. For example, if an actor carries a whip, the audience knows he is outdoors riding a horse.

In Japan, the most popular kind of theater today is kabuki (kah BOO kee). Female dancers acted out the earliest kabuki plays. But later on, men played all the parts.

Peking opera has been the major form of drama in China since the 1800's.

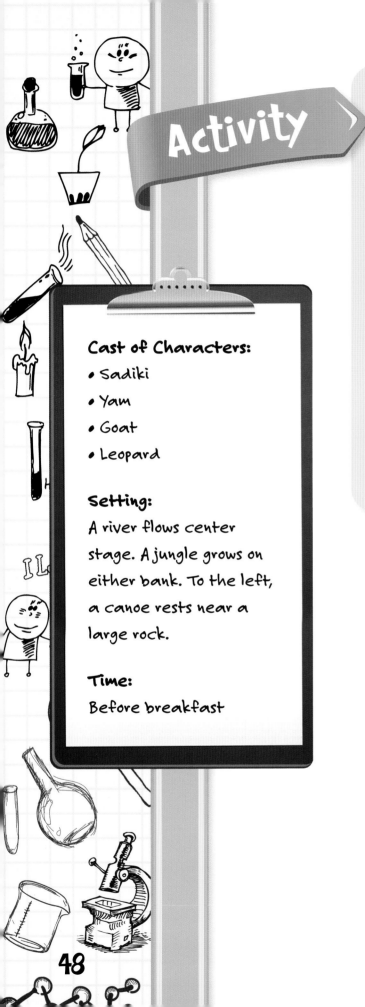

STAGE AN AFRICAN FOLK TALE

Here's a play made from a **folk tale** of the Hausa (HOW sah) people of Africa. Sadiki (sah DEE kee) is a young Hausa man who was kidnapped by enemies and forced to do chores in their village. He manages to escape with his only possessions—a goat, a leopard, and a yam.

Grab a friend or two and pick characters. Take turns reading the lines of the play. On the pages following the script are instructions for how to make costumes.

Cast of Characters:
- Sadiki
- Yam
- Goat
- Leopard

Setting:
A river flows center stage. A jungle grows on either bank. To the left, a canoe rests near a large rock.

Time:
Before breakfast

(The yam rolls to the edge of the river. The leopard leaps onstage followed by Sadiki. The goat ambles in.)

Sadiki: *(resting on the rock and looking nervous)* The sun is up. Soon the villagers will be looking for me.

Goat: But Boss, now you are free and ready to start anew.

Yam: With a yam, a goat, and a leopard. What more could you ask, Boss?

Goat: We need a better head start on the villagers who are after us. Let's board this canoe and put the river between us and them.

Goat: *(studying the canoe)* This small canoe can carry only two of us.

Yam: *(fearfully)* Boss must paddle, so only one of us can go with him.

Sadiki: I shall simply cross the river several times. Will you be first to cross, Yam?

Goat: Oh no, Boss! Then I will be left alone with the leopard, and she will surely eat me.

Sadiki: So the leopard should go first.

Yam: Oh, no, Boss. Then I will be left alone with the goat, and he will surely eat me.

Sadiki: So the goat goes first.

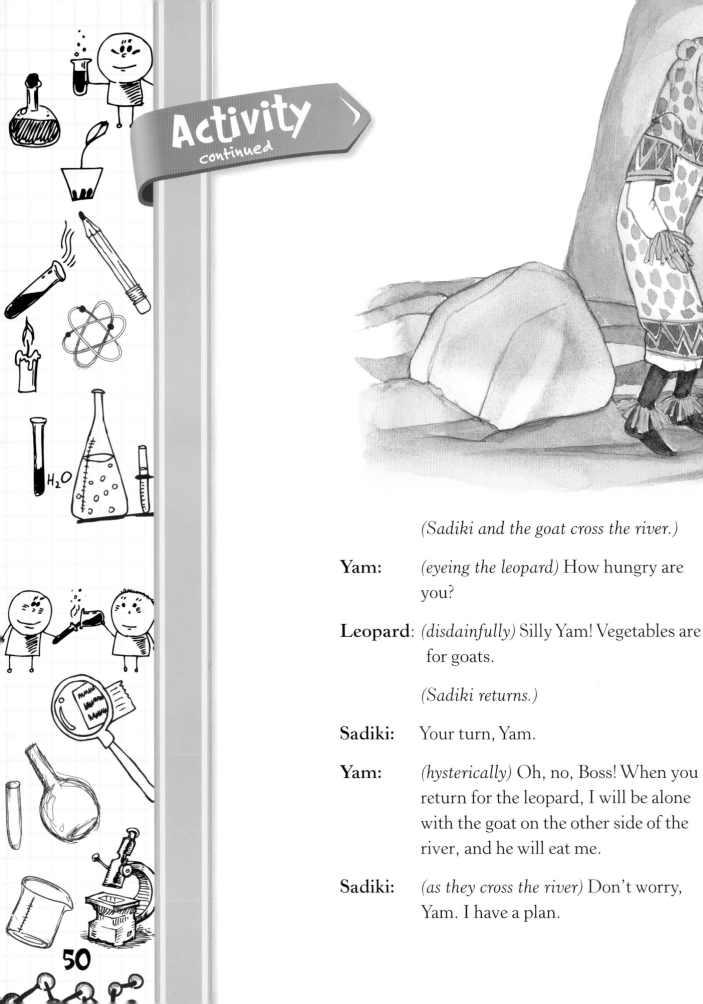

(*Sadiki and the goat cross the river.*)

Yam: (*eyeing the leopard*) How hungry are you?

Leopard: (*disdainfully*) Silly Yam! Vegetables are for goats.

(*Sadiki returns.*)

Sadiki: Your turn, Yam.

Yam: (*hysterically*) Oh, no, Boss! When you return for the leopard, I will be alone with the goat on the other side of the river, and he will eat me.

Sadiki: (*as they cross the river*) Don't worry, Yam. I have a plan.

Goat: *(licking his chops)* Good choice, Boss.

Sadiki: You sly goat, get in the canoe.

(Sadiki and the goat return to the left bank. Sadiki leads the goat out of the canoe.)

Leopard: Yum, here comes my lunch.

Sadiki: Your turn to get in the boat, Leopard.

(The leopard joins the yam on the other side of the river as Sadiki returns a fourth time for the goat.)

Leopard: So Boss figured out how to keep you safe and me hungry.

Yam: *(smugly)* Planning keeps people the masters and us their servants.

MAKE COSTUMES

Follow these directions to make a costume for the Sadiki character in the play you just read.

Sadiki Costume

1. Fold the sheet in half. Pin the T-shirt on the sheet with the neck and sleeves at the fold. Cut the sheet around the shirt. Do not cut the fold at the top of the sheet.

2. Cut out the neck opening. On one side of the costume, cut an 8-inch (20-centimeter) slit from the neck down the center so the costume can slip over Sadiki's head.

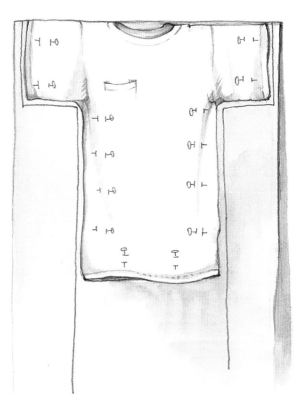

3. Have an adult help you pin the undersides of the sleeves and the sides of the costume together and stitch them up. Then turn the costume inside out so the stitches are hidden.

MATERIALS

- Old white sheet (ask a grown-up for this)
- Extra large T-shirt
- Straight pins
- Scissors
- Needle
- Thread
- Felt-tipped pens
- Ruler

4. With felt-tipped pens, draw a border around the neck, cuffs, and bottom hem. Copy one or more of the African designs shown below.

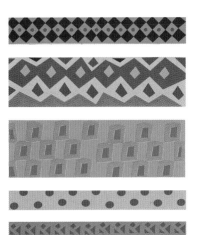

MAKE COSTUMES

Use paper bags for the head gear of the other characters. Make the body costumes the same way you made the Sadiki costume, but color them differently.

MATERIALS

- 3 old white sheets (ask a grown-up for these)
- Extra large T-shirt
- Large paper bags
- Scissors
- Felt-tipped pens
- Face paint
- Glue
- Cardboard
- Yarn
- Cotton balls
- Tape

Leopard Costume

1. Cut a large hole in a bag for the actor's face.

2. Dot the bag with black or brown spots.

3. Draw whiskers and a nose on your face with face paint. Glue cardboard ears to the bag.

4. Use yarn to make funny wristbands.

Goat Costume

1. Cut a large hole in a bag for the actor's face.

2. Glue cardboard ears and a goatee, or little beard, to the bag.

3. Cover the rest of the bag with cotton balls. Allow the glue to dry before using the costume.

Yam Costume

1. Cut a large hole in a bag for the actor's face.

2. Color the bag orange.

3. Tape leaves made of cardboard to the top.

When you look for props, use your imagination. A long, flat box can be a canoe, and a broom can be an oar. A small stool in a large paper bag would make an excellent boulder. Color the bag gray and crumple it a little.

Many Puppets from Many Places

Punch and Judy are the main characters in a type of comic puppet show popular in England.

What kind of performer never needs to know what he or she is going to do or say? A puppet! Although a puppet does not need a script, the puppeteer does. The puppeteer is the person who works the puppet.

Many puppets are hand puppets. One kind of hand puppet is called a glove puppet. It has a head attached to a mittenlike upper body. The puppeteer's hand fits inside the glove. The puppeteer's thumb and fingers move the puppet's arms and head.

A **marionette** (MAR ee uh NEHT) has a whole body, including legs. Most marionettes are moved by strings that run from their head, shoulders, hands, and knees up to the control—a small wooden frame. Puppeteers hide backstage and work the marionettes by moving the controls from above.

A puppeteer controls the movements of his marionette from backstage.

Puppeteers work **rod puppets** by moving rods or sticks. A rod puppet can be just a head mounted on a stick. Or it may have a complete body with movable body parts.

In Japan, rod puppets are used in a form of puppet show called bunraku (buhn RAH koo), or doll theater. A bunraku puppet has joints that move. Its eyes, mouth, and even its eyebrows move, too.

In other parts of Asia, rod puppets perform shadow plays. Strong lights from above and behind cast the puppets' shadows on a cloth screen. The puppets in these shadow plays are often made of leather. In China and Turkey, leather puppets are dyed, and they cast colored shadows.

Wayang kulit is a form of shadow puppet theater that originated in Java, Indonesia. A dramatic story is told using flat, leather puppets that throw their shadows on a screen.

MAKE A SOCK PUPPET

Putting on a puppet show is fun. But first, you have to make your cast of characters.

MATERIALS

- Socks
- Marker
- Buttons
- Needle
- Thread
- Yarn
- Scissors
- Glue

DIRECTIONS

1. Place a sock over your hand. Using a marker, draw a circle where you think the eyes should go.

2. Take the sock off and sew on the buttons for the eyes.

3. If you are using a patterned sock, just adding eyes might be enough to create a character. If so, place the sock back on your hand and push the fabric in between your thumb and forefingers to make a mouth.

58

4. To add hair, cut strands of yarn the length you want the hair to be. Either glue or sew the yarn onto the sock above the eyes.

Now you are ready to put on a performance with your cast of characters!

PUPPET SHOW

STAGE A SHADOW PLAY

Find a coloring book that tells a story. Then turn its characters into **rod puppets** and create a shadow play.

To Make Puppets

1. Find page-sized pictures of people and animals in the coloring book. Tear out each page. Glue each page picture-side-up onto the cardboard.

2. Cut along the outline of the pictures.

3. Tape the end of a pencil to the back of each cutout.

MATERIALS

- Coloring book
- Scissors
- Glue
- Cardboard
- Pencils
- 2 old sheets (ask a grown-up for these)
- Masking tape
- Small table
- Lights or floor lamps
- Card table

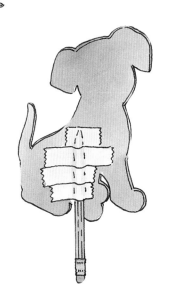

To Make a Screen

Ask an adult to tape an old sheet over a doorway.
Place the card table behind the screen, and
drape the second sheet over the table.

To Put On a Play

1. Make up lines, or words, for each character to
   say. Be sure the lines tell a story.

2. Turn on lights in the room behind the screen.

3. Crouch down behind the table. Lift each puppet
   by the pencil on its back. Make sure that the
   light shines behind the puppet and casts its
   shadow on the screen. Remember to change
   your voice for each puppet when you say its lines!

Glossary

batik an Indonesian method of printing fabric by painting parts with wax and then dyeing the fabric.

brass a family of musical instruments made of metal and played by blowing into a cup-shaped mouthpiece. The trumpet, trombone, and French horn are brasses.

embroidery; embroider the art of making decorations with needlework; to make an ornamental design or pattern on cloth, leather, or other material, with stitches.

folk dance the traditional form of social dancing of a nation or ethnic group.

folk tale a story or legend originating and handed down among the common people.

marionette a puppet with jointed arms and legs that are moved with strings or wires.

origami the Asian craft of paper folding.

papier-mâché a light, strong molding material made of paper pulp and glue.

percussion a family of musical instruments that make music when struck, such as drums.

piñata a decoration filled with candy and other treats, used especially in Latin American festivities.

pottery pots, dishes, or vases made from clay and hardened by heat.

rod puppet a puppet that is operated by rods or sticks, usually from below the stage.

Find Out More

Books

Clay by Anna Llimós Plomer (Gareth Stevens Publishing, 2003)

The Jumbo Book of Drama by Deborah Dunleavy and Jane Kurisu (Kids Can Press, 2004)

Making Basic Origami Shapes Step by Step by Michael G. LaFosse (PowerKids Press, 2002)

Mexico and Central America: A Fiesta of Culture, Crafts, and Activities for Ages 8-12 by Mary Turck (Chicago Review Press, 2004)

Puppets by Meryl Doney (Gareth Stevens Publishing, 2004)

The Quilting Bee by Gail Gibbons (HarperCollins Publishers, 2004)

Websites

AuntAnnie.com: Crafts and More, for All Ages!
http://www.auntannie.com/
Instructions for a wide variety of projects are available at this website.

Family Fun: Crafts By Type
http://familyfun.go.com/crafts/crafts-by-type/
Look for art and sewing projects, make your own musical instruments, put together costumes and more at this website.

Hands-On Crafts
http://www.handsoncrafts.org/000-a.htm
Play around with pottery projects at this website, which also features quilting, weaving, and basket-making.

The Idea Box: Crafts
http://www.theideabox.com/Craft_list.html
Hundreds of craft projects are listed alphabetically on this site, which features crafts for kids of all ages.

Kinder Art: Sculpture Lessons and Activities
http://www.kinderart.com/sculpture/
Try your hand at different sculpture projects, from clay pots to tiles, masks, and even gargoyles.

SFS Kids: Fun with Music!
http://www.sfskids.org/templates/splash.asp
This website from the San Francisco Symphony orchestra includes a music lab, features on different musical instruments, and a selection of radio stations for young listeners.

Young Embroiderers
http://www.hiraeth.com/ytg/proj_index.htm
Take a look at sewing and embroidery projects from the Young Embroiderers' Club.

Index

Activities